POLITICAL VIEW

POLITICAL VIEW

TAMANA TAMANA

ISBN 979-888606790-3

Contents

Acknowledgements

• Acknowledgment
A variety of methods are deployed in politics, which include promoting one's own political views among people, negotiation with other political subjects, making laws, and exercising force, including warfare against adversaries. ... In modern nation states, people often form political parties to represent their ideas The relationship between politics and society is more complex than ever due to **the emergence of new power structures, forms of conflict organization and management, and social practices of political participation**

CHAPTER ONE

- **Politics** (from <u>Greek</u>: *Πολιτικά, politiká*, 'affairs of the cities') is the method of <u>ruler ship</u> over a <u>national government</u>, <u>state government</u> and <u>local government</u> in <u>groups</u>, or other forms of <u>ruling power relations</u> among individuals, such as the distribution of <u>resources</u> or <u>status</u>. The branch of <u>social science</u> that studies <u>ruler ship</u>, <u>law making</u> and <u>government</u> is referred to as <u>political science</u>.

It may be used positively in the context of a "political solution" which is compromising and nonviolent, or descriptively as "the art or science of government", but also often carries a negative connotation. For example, abolitionist <u>Wendell Phillips</u> declared that "we do not play politics; <u>anti-slavery</u> is no half-jest with us The concept has been defined in various ways, and different approaches have fundamentally differing views on whether it should be used extensively or limitedly, empirically or normatively, and on whether conflict or co-operation is more essential to it.

A variety of methods are deployed in politics, which include promoting one's own political views among people, <u>negotiation</u> with other political subjects, making <u>laws</u>, and exercising <u>force</u>, including <u>warfare</u> against adversaries. Politics is exercised on a wide range of social levels, from clans and tribes of traditional societies, through modern local governments, companies and institutions up to sovereign states, to the international level. In modern nation states, people often form political parties to represent their ideas. Members of a party often agree to take the same position on many issues and agree to support the same changes to law and the same leaders. An election is usually a competition between different parties.

A political system is a framework which defines acceptable political methods within a society. The history of political thought can be traced back to early antiquity, with seminal works such as Plato's *Republic* and Aristotle's *Politics* in the West, and Confucius's political manuscripts and Chanakya's *Arthashastra* in the East.

The English *politics* has its roots in the name of Aristotle's classic work, *Politiká*, which introduced the Greek term *politiká* (*Πολιτικά*, 'affairs of the cities'). In the mid-15th century, Aristotle's composition would be rendered in Early Modern English as *Polettiques* [sic],[a][11] which would become *Politics* in Modern English.

The singular *politic* first attested in English in 1430, coming from Middle French*politique*—itself taking from *politicus*,[12] a Latinization of the Greek *πολιτικός* (*politikos*) from *πολίτης* (*polites*, 'citizen') and *πόλις* (*polis*, 'city')

- In the view of Harold Laswell, politics is "who gets what, when, how.
- For David Easton, it is about "the authoritative allocation of values for a society.

- To <u>Vladimir Lenin</u>, "politics is the most concentrated expression of economics.
- <u>Bernard Crick</u> argued that "politics is a distinctive form of rule whereby people act together through institutionalized procedures to resolve differences, to conciliate diverse interests and values and to make public policies in the pursuit of common purposes.
- According to <u>Adrian Leftish</u> "Politics comprises all the activities of co-operation, negotiation and conflict within and between societies, whereby people go about organizing the use, production or distribution of human, natural and other resources in the course of the production and reproduction of their biological and social life.
- Politics is the sphere of activity involved in running a state. According to Max Webber the "state can be defined as a human community that successfully claims the monopoly of the legitimate use of physical force within a given
- <u>Adrian Leftish</u> has differentiated views of politics based on how extensive or limited their perception of what accounts as 'political' is The extensive view sees politics as present across the sphere of human social relations, while the limited view restricts it to certain contexts. For example, in a more restrictive way, politics may be viewed as primarily about <u>governance</u>, while a <u>feminist perspective</u> could argue that sites which have been viewed traditionally as non-political, should indeed be viewed as political as well.[1] This latter position is encapsulated in the slogan *the personal is political*, which disputes the distinction between private and public issues. Instead, politics may be defined by the use of power, as has been argued by <u>Robert A. Dahl</u>.

- **Moralism and realism**
- Some perspectives on politics view it empirically as an exercise of power, while others see it as a social function with a <u>normative</u> basis.[1] This distinction has been called the difference between <u>political *moralism*</u> and <u>political *realism*</u>.[1] For moralists, politics is closely linked to <u>ethics</u>, and is at its extreme in <u>utopian</u> thinking. For example, according to <u>Hannah Arendt</u>, the view of <u>Aristotle</u> was that "to be political...meant that everything was decided through words and persuasion and not through violence; while according to <u>Bernard Crick</u> "[p]politics is the way in which free societies are governed. Politics is politics and other forms of rule are something else. In contrast, for realists, represented by those such as <u>Niccolò Machiavelli</u>, <u>Thomas Hobbes</u>, and <u>Harold Laswell</u>, politics is based on the use of power, irrespective of the ends being pursued.
- **Conflict and co-operation**
- <u>Ageism</u> argues that politics essentially comes down to conflict between conflicting interests. Political scientist Elmer Schattschneider argued that "at the root of all politics is the universal language of conflict, while for <u>Carl Schmitt</u> the essence of politics is the distinction of 'friend' from foe'. This is in direct contrast to the more co-operative views of politics by Aristotle and Crick. However, a more mixed view between these extremes is provided by Irish political scientist Michael Laver, who noted that:
- Politics is about the characteristic blend of conflict and co-operation that can be found so often in human interactions. Pure conflict is war. Pure co-operation is true love. Politics is a mixture of both.

- His political history of the <u>world</u> is the history of the various <u>political entities</u> created by the <u>human race</u> throughout their existence and the way these states define their borders. Throughout <u>history</u>, political systems have expanded from basic systems of <u>self-governance</u> and <u>monarchy</u> to the complex <u>democratic</u> and totalitarian systems that exist today. In parallel, political entities have expanded from vaguely defined frontier-type <u>boundaries</u>, to the national definite boundaries existing today

The early distribution of political power was determined by the availability of <u>fresh water</u>, <u>fertile soil</u>, and <u>temperate climate</u> of different locations. These were all necessary for the development of highly organized societies. The locations of these early societies were near, or benefiting from, the edges of <u>tectonic plates</u> the <u>Indus Valley Civilization</u> was located next to the Himalayas (which were created by tectonic pressures) and the Indus and Ganges rivers, which deposit sediment from the mountains to produce fertile land.[1] A similar dynamic existed in <u>Mesopotamia</u>, where the <u>Tigris</u> and <u>Euphrates</u> did the same with the <u>Zagros Mountains</u>. <u>Ancient Egypt</u> was helped by the <u>Nile</u> depositing sediments from the East African highlands of its origins, while the <u>Yellow River</u> and <u>Yangtze</u> acted in the same way for Ancient China. Eurasia was advantaged in the development of agriculture by the natural occurrence of domestic able wild grass species and the east-west orientation of the landmass, allowing for the easy spread of domesticated crops. A similar advantage was given to it by half of the world's large mammal species living there, which could be domesticated.[1]

The development of agriculture allowed higher populations, with the newly dense and settled societies becoming hierarchical, with inequalities in wealth and freedom.[1] As the cooling and drying of the climate by 3800 BCE caused drought in Mesopotamia, village farmers began co-operating and started creating larger settlements with irrigation systems. This new water infrastructure in turn required centralized administration with complex social organization. The first cities and systems of greater social organization emerged in Mesopotamia, followed within a few centuries by ones at the Indus and Yellow River Valleys. In the cities, the workforce could specialize as the whole population did not have to work for food production, while stored food allowed for large armies to create empires. The first empires were those of Ancient Egypt and Mesopotamia. Smaller kingdoms existed in North China Plain, Indo-Gangetic Plain, Central Asia, Anatolia, Eastern Mediterranean, and Central America, while the rest of humanity continued to live in small tribes.

The first states of sorts were those of early dynastic Sumer and early dynastic Egypt, which arose from the auk and Predynastic Egypt respectively at approximately 3000BCE. Early dynastic Egypt was based around the Nile River in the north-east of Africa, the kingdom's boundaries being based around the Nile and stretching to areas where oases existed.[1]Upper and Lower Egypt were unified around 3150 BCE by Pharaoh Menes. This process of consolidation was driven by the crowding of migrants from the expanding Sahara in the Nile delta.[20] Nevertheless, political competition continued within the country between centers of power such as Memphis and Thebes. The prevailing n The geopolitical environment of the Egyptians had them surrounded by <u>Nubia</u> in the smaller southern oases of the Nile unreachable by boat, as well as by Libyan warlords operating from the oases around modern-day <u>Benghazi</u>, and finally by raiders across the <u>Sinai</u> and the sea. The country was well defended by natural barriers formed by the Sahara on both sides, though this also limited its ability to expand into a larger empire, mostly remaining a regional power along the Nile (except for a conquest of the Levant in the second millennium BCE). The lack of timber also made it too expensive to build a large navy for power projection across the Mediterranean or Red Seas

Mesopotamian dominance

Mesopotamia is situated between the major rivers of <u>Tigris</u> and <u>Euphrates</u>, and the first political power in the region was the <u>Akkadian Empire</u> starting around 2300 BCE.[22] They were later followed by <u>Sumer</u>, <u>Babylon</u>, and <u>Assyria</u>. They faced competition from the mountainous areas to the north, strategically positioned above the Mesopotamian plains, with kingdoms such as <u>Mitanni</u>, <u>Urartu</u>, <u>Elam</u>, and <u>Medes</u>. The Mesopotamians also innovated in governance by writing the first laws.

A dry climate in the Iron Age caused turmoil as movements of people put pressure on the existing states resulting in the <u>Late Bronze Age collapse</u>, with <u>Cimmerians</u>, <u>Arameans</u>, <u>Dorians</u>, and the <u>Sea Peoples</u> migrating among others. Babylon never recovered following the death of <u>Hammurabi</u> in 1699 BCE. Following this, <u>Assyria</u> grew in power under <u>Adad-nirari II</u> By the late ninth century BCE, the Assyrian Empire controlled almost all of Mesopotamia and much of the <u>Levant</u> and <u>Anatolia</u>. Meanwhile, Egypt was weakened, eventually breaking apart after the death of <u>Osorkon II</u> until 710 BCE. In 853, the Assyrians fought and won a battle against a coalition of Babylon, Egypt, Persia, Israel, Aram, and ten other nations, with over 60,000 troops taking part according to contemporary sources. However, the empire was weakened by internal struggles for power, and was plunged into a decade of turmoil beginning with a plague in 763 BCE. Following revolts by cities and lesser kingdoms against the empire, a <u>coup d'état</u> was staged in 745 by <u>Tiglath- Pileser III</u>. He raised the army from 44,000 to 72,000, followed by his successor <u>Sennacherib</u> who raised it to 208,000, and finally by <u>Ashurbanipal</u> who raised an army of over 300,000.[1] This allowed the empire to spread over <u>Cyprus</u>, the entire <u>Levant</u>, <u>Phrygia</u>, <u>Urartu</u>, <u>Cimmerians</u>, <u>Persia</u>, <u>Medes</u>, <u>Elam</u>, and <u>Babylon</u>.

Persian dominance

By 650, Assyria had started declining as a severe drought hit the Middle East and an alliance was formed against them.[1] Eventually they were replaced by the <u>Median empire</u> as the main power of the region following the <u>Battle of Carchemish</u> (605) and the <u>Battle of the Eclipse</u> (585) The Medians served as the launching pad for the rise of the <u>Persian Empire</u>.[1] After first serving as vassals, under the third Persian king <u>Cambyses I</u> their influence rose, and in 553 they rose against the Medians. By the death of <u>Cyrus the Great</u>, the Persian <u>Achaemenes Empire</u> reached from <u>Aegean Sea</u> to <u>Indus River</u> and <u>Caucasus</u> to <u>Nubia</u>. The empire was divided into provinces ruled by <u>satraps</u>, who collected taxes and were typically local power brokers The empire controlled about a third of the world's farm land and a quarter of its population. In 522, after King

<u>Cambyses II's</u> death, <u>Darius the Great</u> took over power

Greek dominance

As the population of <u>Ancient Greece</u> grew, they began a colonization of the Mediterranean region.[37] This encouraged trade, which in turn caused political changes in the city-states with old elites being overthrown in <u>Corinth</u> in 657 and in <u>Athens</u> in 632, for example.[38] There were many wars between the cities as well, including the <u>Messenian Wars</u> (743-742; 685-668), the <u>Levantine War</u> (710-650), and the <u>First Sacred War</u> (595-585).[38] In the seventh and sixth centuries, Corinth and <u>Sparta</u> were the dominant powers of Greece.[39] The former was eventually supplanted by Athens as the main sea power, while Sparta remained the dominant land-force.[40] In 499, in the <u>Ionian Revolt</u> Greek cities in Asia Minor rebelled against the Persian Empire but were crushed in the <u>Battle of Lade</u>.[41] After this, the Persians invaded the Greek mainland in the <u>Greco-Persian Wars</u> (499-449).[41]

The <u>Macedonian</u> King <u>Philip II</u> (350-336) conquered much of Greece.[42] In 338, he formed the <u>League of Corinth</u> to liberate Greeks in Asia Minor from the Persians, with 10,000 troops invading in 336.[42] After his murder, his son <u>Alexander the Great</u> took charge and crossed the <u>Dardanelles</u> in 334.[43] After Asia Minor had been conquered, Alexander invaded Levant, Egypt, and Mesopotamia, defeating the Persians under <u>Darius the Great</u> in the <u>Battle of Gaugamela</u> in 331, and ending the last resistance by 328.[43] After Alexander's death in Babylon in 323, the empire had no designated successor.[44] This led to its division into four: the <u>Antigonid dynasty</u> in <u>Macedonia</u>, the <u>Attalid dynasty</u> in <u>Anatolia</u>, the <u>Ptolemaic Kingdom</u> in <u>Egypt</u>, and the

Seleucid Empire over Mesopotamia.[45]

Roman dominance [edit]

Rome became dominant in the Mediterranean in the 3rd century BC after defeating the Samnite's, the Gauls and the Etruscans for control of the Italian Peninsula.[46] In 264, it challenged its main rival Carthage to a fight for Sicily, starting the Punic Wars.[47] A truce was signed in 241, with Rome gaining Corsica and Sardinia in addition to Sicily.[47] In 218, the Carthaginian general Hannibal marched out of Spain towards Italy, crossing the Alps with his war elephants.[48] After 15 years of fighting, the Romans beat him and then sent troops against Carthage itself, defeating it in 202.[49] The Second Punic War alone cost Rome 100,000 casualties.[50] In 146, Carthage was finally destroyed completely.[51]

Rome suffered from various internal disturbances and instabilities. In 133, Tiberius Gracchus was killed alongside hundreds of supporters after trying to redistribute public land to the poor.[52] The Social War (91-88) was caused by neighboring cities trying to secure themselves the benefits of Roman citizenship.[52] In 82, General Sulla captured power violently, ending the Roman Republic and becoming a dictator.[53] Following his death new power struggles emerged, and in Caesar's Civil War (49-46), Julius Caesar and Pompey fought over the empire, with the former winning.[54] After the ruler was assassinated in 44, a second civil war broke out between his potential heirs, Mark Antony and Augustus, the latter becoming emperor.[54] This then led to the *Pax Romana*, a long period of peace in the empire.[55] The quarrels between the Ptolemaic Kingdom, the Seleucid Empire, the Parthian Empire and the Kingdom of Pontus in the Near East allowed the

Romans to expand up to the Euphrates.[42] During Augustus' reign the Rhine, Danube, and the Sahara became the other borders of the empire.[56] The population reached about 60 million.[57]

Political instability in Rome grew. Emperor Caligula (37-41) was murdered by the Praetorian Guard to replace him with Claudius (41-53), while his successor Nero (54-68) burned Rome down.[58] The average reign from his death to Philip the Arab (244-249) was six years.[58] Nevertheless, external expansion continued, with Trajan (98-117) invading Dacia, Parthia and Arabia.[59] Its only formidable enemy was the Parthian Empire.[60] Migrating peoples started exerting pressure on the borders of the empire.[61] The drying climate of Central Asia forced the Huns to move, and in 370 they crossed Don and soon after the Danube, forcing the Goths on the move, which in turn caused other Germanic tribes to overrun Roman borders.[62] In 293, Diocletian (284-305) appointed three rulers for different parts of the empire.[63] It was formally divided in 395 by Theodosius I (379-395) into the Western Roman and Byzantine Empires.[64] In 406 the northern border of the former was overrun by the Alemannia, Vandals and Suebi invaded.[65] In 408 the Visigoths invaded Italy and then sacked Rome in 410.[65] The final collapse of the Western Empire came in 476 with the deposal of Romulus August ulus (475-476

Indian subcontinent

.Built around the Indus River, by 2500 BCE the Indus Valley Civilization, located in modern-day India, Pakistan and Afghanistan, had formed. The civilization's boundaries extended to 600 km from the Arabian Sea.[67] After its cities Mohenjo-daro and Harappa were abandoned around 1900 BCE, no political power known to have replaced it.[68]

States began to form in 12th century BCE with the formation of Kuru Kingdom which was first state level administration in Indian subcontinent. In 6th century BCE with the emergence of Mahajanapadas.[69] Out of sixteen such states, four strong ones emerged: Kosala, Magadha, Vatsa, and Avanti, with Magadha dominating the rest by the mid-fifth century.[70] The Magadha then transformed into the Nanda Empire under Mahapadma Nanda (345-321), extending from the Gangetic plains to the Hindu Kush and the Deccan Plateau.[71] The empire was, however, overtaken by Chandragupta Maurya (324-298), turning it into the Maurya Empire.[71] He defended against Alexander's invasion from the West and received control of the Hindu Kush mountain passes in a peace treaty signed in 303.[71]By the time of his grandson Ashoka's rule, the empire stretched from Zagros Mountains to the Brahmaputra River.[72] The empire contained a population of 50 to 60 million, governed by a system of provinces ruled by governor-princes, with a capital in Pataliputra.[73]

After Ashoka's death, the empire had begun to decline, with Kashmir in the north, Shunga and Satavahana in the center, and Kalinga as well as Pandya in the south becoming independent. In to this power vacuum, the Yuezhi were able to establish the new Kushan Empire in 30 CE. The Gupta Empire was founded by Chandragupta I (320-335), which in sixty years expanded from the Ganges to the Bay of Bengal and the Indus River following the downfall of the Kushan Empire.[Gupta governance was similar to that of the Maurya.[Following wars with the Hephthalites and other problems, the empire fell by 550

China

See also: Ancient China

In the North China Plain, the Yellow River allowed the rise of states such as Wei and Qi.[79] This area was first unified by the Shang dynasty around 1600 BCE, and replaced by the Zhou dynasty in the Battle of Muye in 1046 BCE, with reportedly millions taking part in the fighting.[79] The victors were however hit by internal unrest soon after.[80] The main rivals of the Zhou were the Dongyi in Shandong, the Xianyun in Ordos, the Guifang in Shanxi, as well as the Chu in the middle reaches of the Yangtze.

Beginning in the eighth century BCE China fell into a state of anarchy for five centuries during the Spring and Autumn (771-476) and Warring States periods (476-221).[82] During the latter period, the Jin dynasty split into the Wei, Zhao and Han states, while the rest of the North China Plain was composed of the Chu, Qin, Qi and Yan states, while the Zhou remained in the center with largely ceremonial power.[83] While the Zhao had an advantage at first, the Qin ended up defeating them in 260 with about half a million soldiers fighting on each side at the Battle of Changping.[84] The other states tried to form an alliance against the Qin but were defeated.[85] In 221, the Qin dynasty was established with a population of about 40 million, with a capital of 350,000 in Linzi.[86] Under the leadership of Qin Shi Huang, the dynasty initiated reforms such as establishing territorial administrative units, infrastructure projects (including the Great Wall of China) and uniform Chinese characters.[87]However, after his death and burial with the Terracotta Army, the empire started falling apart when the Chu and Han started fighting over a power vacuum left by a weak heir, with the Han dynasty rising to power in 204 BCE.[88]

Under the Han, the population of China rose to 50 million, with 400,000 in the capital Chang'an, and with territorial expansion to Korea, Vietnam and Tien Shan.[89] Expeditions were also sent against the Xiongnu and to secure the Hexi Corridor, the Nanyue kingdom was annexed, and Hainan and Taiwan conquered.[90] The Chinese pressure on the Xiongnu forced them towards the west, leading to the exodus of the Yuezhi, who in turn pillaged the capital of Bactria.[91] This then led to their new Kushan Empire.[75] The end of the Han dynasty came following internal upheavals in 220 CE, with its split into the Shu, Wu and Wei states.[42] Despite the rise of the Jin dynasty (266–420), China was soon invaded by the Xiongnu in the rebellion of the Five Barbarians (304-316), who conquered large areas of the Northern China plain and declared the Northern Wei in 399

Americas

The Tiwanaku Politypolity in western Bolivia based in the southern Lake Titicaca Basin. Its influence extended into present-day Peru and Chile and lasted from around 600 to 1000 AD.[99]Chimor was the political grouping of the Chimú culture that ruled the northern coast of Peru beginning around 850 and ending around 1470. Chimor was the largest kingdom in the Late Intermediate period, encompassing 1,000 kilometres (620 mi) of coastline. The Aymara kingdoms in turn were a group of native polities that flourished towards the Late Intermediate Period, after the fall of the Tiwanaku Empire, whose societies were geographically located in the <u>Qullaw</u>. They were developed between 1150 and 1477, before the kingdoms disappeared due to the military conquest of the <u>Inca Empire</u>.

Beginning around 250 AD, the <u>Maya civilization</u> develop many <u>city-states</u> linked by a complex <u>trade network</u>. In the Maya Lowlands two great rivals, the cities of <u>Tikal</u> and <u>Calakmul</u>, became powerful. The period also saw the intrusive intervention of the central Mexican city of <u>Teotihuacan</u> in Maya dynasti